POETRY now

MY ETERNAL LOVE

Edited by

Heather Killingray

First published in Great Britain in 1999 by
POETRY NOW
Remus House, Coltsfoot Drive,
Woodston,
Peterborough, PE2 9JX
Telephone (01733) 898101
Fax (01733) 313524

HB ISBN 0 75430 634 8
SB ISBN 0 75430 635 6

FOREWORD

Although we are a nation of poetry writers we are accused of not reading poetry and not buying poetry books: after many years of listening to the incessant gripes of poetry publishers, I can only assume that the books they publish, in general, are books that most people do not want to read.

Poetry should not be obscure, introverted, and as cryptic as a crossword puzzle: it is the poet's duty to reach out and embrace the world.

The world owes the poet nothing and we should not be expected to dig and delve into a rambling discourse searching for some inner meaning.

The reason we write poetry (and almost all of us do) is because we want to communicate: an ideal; an idea; or a specific feeling.

Poetry is as essential in communication, as a letter; a radio; a telephone, and the main criteria for selecting the poems in this anthology is very simple: they communicate.

CONTENTS

CAMBRIDGE RAILWAY STATION AUTUMN 1980

I did not stay long, preferring the swift rupture to
slow disappearance on shining rails a mile away and then
a thousand and another thousand towards the vast Americas.
If the platform there could speak, would speak and if could cry,
would cry at dramas plotted there, including this.
The soldier on his way to death on foreign field from
this fair city but this death (as then it seemed) left
no corpse, two living victims, one in speeding train and
one remaining there, yet those around felt not the violence
nor heard the cracking of the calm.
I tell you they neither felt nor heard.

R L Clifford

THE PERFECT DREAM

There was a land of perfect peace
Created in my dream,
With rolling hills and daffodils
And bubbling silver streams.
Every morn the sun would rise,
Always clear and bright,
The stars glittered in the sky,
All through the hours of night.
The arch of every rainbow
Led to a pot of gold,
And every flower brought to life
The truth within my soul.
Every note of music played
Was beautiful to hear,
And if the rain should ever fall
The air was left so clear.
This was all a perfect dream -
A dream that's now come true.
It's all I've ever wanted
To share my life with you.

L A Ereira

YET STILL

Do you love me, she oft asks.
Do I love my beating heart
Or my good right arm,
They are, she is
forever now a part of me.
I love her as my thirst loves drink
Or my hunger sustenance,
I am; she is, a single whole,
We are a one in love
Caring for the only one,
Four arms, four legs, two heads.
She is I and I am she
Joined as an entity,
Safe from the surgeon's knife,
Yet still she asks,
Do you love me still?

Richard Reeve

ODE TO THE ONE I LOVE

I will love you always,
and always I'll be true,
always I will love you,
I'll love only you.

Say you'll love me always,
say you'll always care,
we can walk life's path together,
all the good times, bad times share.

I will love you always.
Say always you'll be mine,
we can sail life's storms together,
and bask in love's sunshine.

Heaven will know no bounds,
for a love so true.
That's if you'll always love me
as much as I love you.

Always I will love you,
even more with passing time,
I will love you always,
say forever you'll be mine.

Patricia Lynne Phipps

NEW GUINEA

Many years ago we joined a trek
My mother and I
In that 'wild' and distant island
Full of undiscovered tribes
(And undiscovered love).
Walked from the island's centre
South to the coast's hot summer,
Escorted by an Australian ranger.

Natives thought my mother
At sixty years was ancient
So venerated her all the way
But for me - the ranger - a holiday romance.
Kind and thoughtful and no demands
But married with a son.

I was free but cautious yet
And so remained quite chaste.
Perhaps he was my one true love.
To him I was a 'one night stand'.
Would have denied it all.
But never cheated me with lies.

All I thought, ate, lived and breathed was him
Knowing his face I'd not forget.
A quarter of a century has passed
And still I can recall
Every word and every smile
Locked deep within my heart.

T B Smith

JUST A GAME

If breaking my heart, was all you could do.
Then why did you, want me to make love to you.
Last night you came, and asked me to stay.
Now you watch as I turn away.
Was nothing meant by last night,
Nor, the tears you cry.
Love's not just a game we play,
We can't just kiss, and run away.

Love can be a passionate flower,
Coming to life, in an hour.
My heart's blossomed for you.
That's why, I made love to you.
Last night's events, were forbidden,
True feelings deeply hidden.
Love's not just a game to play,
We can't just kiss, and turn away.

After all we have said and done,
I'm wishing we had never begun.
Last night you came, breaking my heart,
Because of that we have to part.
Our love was forbidden,
Never to happen.
Love's never just a game to play.
For no one kisses, just to run away.

Ian Littlewood

LOVE TIMES

Who would have thought
That I would find
The love that I was searching for
In so short a space of time.

The loves that I have known before
Have paled against the sun.
You brought the sparkle to my eyes,
I knew the future had begun.

The best of everything I am
I'll keep to give to you,
That in the fullness of our lives
We might know this love is true.

Whatever fate holds in her hand
Can never harm a love this strong,
I'll wait, and hope, and pray that you
Will find the heart where you belong.

Fiona J Saunders

MISSING YOU

I miss you so my darling
more than you will ever know
I'm so lost without your loving
no cuddles, no kisses, no looks

To speak to you is wonderful for just a little while
it makes me feel so happy and uplifted
each day my life feels empty, I miss your loving smile
your voice saying that you love me, your caring tender eyes

I'm longing for your presence
to see your happy face
you'll make my life so right again, help everything make sense
your arms so warm and loving, contentment pure and sweet

The time will soon be over for us to be apart
the wings of love will hover and guide you back to me
I'll then be able to give you all the love that's in my heart
our souls will join together, our thoughts and minds unite.

Sandra Bond

Master Of Fantasy, Mistress Of Reality

I'm the Master of our Fantasy, will it ever end?
Mistress of Reality, just what do you intend.?
We get pleasure from our fantasy, something we can share
It's a secret pleasure, it shows that we both care.

Will it last forever more, or one day come true?
Mistress of Reality, you know that's up to you.
Reality or Fantasy, the choice is yours to make
Reality or Fantasy, which road shall we take?

As we know what special means, whichever way you choose
Our secret will be safe with us, nobody will lose.
Mistress of Reality, please think hard and long
You control our destiny, it's the singer not the song.

R Miles

BLEAK

Bleakness,
enveloping me like the
very bitterness inside.
A world with no soul.
A heartless, care less world.
And an overwhelming feeling that
love should've been mine by now:
was at my fingertips,
is out of reach.
Why is the story
always the same.
I've got to leave my home soon.
I don't know
what to do
or where to go.
Leave.
Leaving.
He's leaving me.

Julia Burton

LOVE'S EMBERS

I waited for the days to melt away
In soft September's russet residue,
And, hearing autumn music, thought of you,
And ventured where our love had gone astray.

In soft September's russet residue
My heart envisioned more than I can say,
And ventured where our love had gone astray,
As if its yearning would make all things new.

My heart envisioned more than I can say,
Still beating where forgotten fancies blew,
As if its yearning would make all things new,
And touch love's embers with some covert ray.

Still beating where forgotten fancies blew,
My heart would epitaph life's troubled way,
And touch love's embers with some covert ray
To put to flight the destiny we knew.

S H Smith

FIRST LOVE

Frenetic activity distracts
Eclectic magpie
Alluring attractions
Shiny currency
Glittering trinkets
Lustrous interiors
Shimmering screens
Glossy pages, tinfoil people
Metallic nomads passing
And brassy clashing airwaves.

Scales fall, dross exposed
As piercing gaze recalls
Brightest light ever
Total illumination
Flashing forth fire
On gilt-laden pages
Most captivating person
Wondrous voice
Engages my return
To my first love
Crucible for my cold heart.

Helen Dean

THE DEPTH OF LOVE

At what time in our life do we appreciate each other as we really are.
For sadly many have undergone surgery, and most some kind of upset
    so as to leave a physical or mental scar.
Our early aspirations are not always ready to accept each other,
    warts and all.
And selfishly and romantically there's an illusion that life will
    always be a ball.
But the saying regarding when the gilt goes off the gingerbread,
    could somehow apply.
And inevitably things are as they are, - that we cannot alter no matter
    how we try.
So that understanding and compassion will call for an inward reserve.
For having spent years of pleasure with someone of our choice
    it's no more than they deserve.
So the time comes for one to depend on the other that inner strength
    they must employ.
There'll be a need to concentrate on just simple pleasures that they
    both enjoy.
It will not be easy to be looked after or for the one who gives the care.
And for there not to be a little resentment from both that this should
    happen would be very rare.
Now exotic holidays and even more modest pleasures will be in
    the past.
But how precious one's company is will be realised and priceless time
    spent alongside each other will be there until the last.

Reg Morris

STEPHEN

Shaggy dark hair, fair skin, strong body,
you were my fantasy on heat wave summer nights.

I breathed you in with garden-scented air,
thought I saw you everywhere;

drank you with coffee,
used your phrases in my speech.

And I believe I was yours until you left,
at sensuous summer's end.

In cruel, frost-fingered January,
I remember you.

Carole Luke

My First And Last Love

Being with you makes me so happy inside, you know by your rules
I'll always abide
The way you look at me, makes me feel so good, I would give you
the world if I could
In your arms I feel sheltered from any harm
I feel the luckiest person when we're walking arm in arm
Nothing you could do, would make me feel sad
If we stay together through all the trials of life
I would be happy to one day become your wife.

Ann Grimwood

L'AMOUR

I love you with every bated breath I breath
I feel you and I have an intense need
I want to feel your pulse, your passion, your seed
To implant me before I bleed.

I want to be as one with your world
I want to hear your truth of how you feel
I want to peak to high levels of sexuality and be real
I want to be your unity seal

I feel the urge of your caress
I need to leave this world and reach points beyond other
I want to reach my fantasies and discover
The world found within my lover

I need to share your intimate thoughts
And leave our bodies entwined as one
To create a new sense of meaning and see what our love has become.

Nigel

BLIND DATE

He came to me by way of a joke
Tommie my blind date from down the street
It was love at first sight the moment he spoke
Trembling knees pumping heart skips a beat
Country pub so quaint a roaring open fire
Holding hands lover's eyes meet composer must contain
Lovely words he speaks sensing his overwhelming desire
Holding hands beneath the table longing to remain
Two new lovers surrounded with bliss
In sweet scented woods to lie this warm summer season
In this man's arms what more could I wish
Contented so happy needing no other reason
Only to be with him my beloved perfect mate
Parting brings nothing but loneliness nausea pain
Wretched lonely days seems forever my wait
For my lover's kisses to lie in his arms again
Under my pillow letters so sweet he leaves for me
Romantic sentences loving poems words just so tender
Wrapped around with pretty pink ribbon just for me to see
So my darling for you I give my heart soul in total surrender

Ann Hathaway

THE HOTS

You make me go crimson
of which I deplore
I do wish to see you
but red-faced no more

It's not just my face
my stomach's in knots
all of these feelings
'cause I've got the hots

My thoughts are all murky
but most of all hazy
I'm thinking of you
and it makes me feel crazy

I dream of your kisses
and how they would feel
maybe one day
I'll get them for real

I think of you constant
to the point of despair.
Why can't you love me
it just isn't fair.

Together a couple
I think we should be
I've got the hots
now have them for me.

Lucy O'Toole

CRUEL LOVE

I knew I was in love with her,
I longed to have her by my side.
But I kept quiet about it all,
My feelings I had to hide.

To her I was just a friend
And that's as far as it went
No candlelit romance
No Valentine's card sent.

She only had eyes for him
That was plain to see
But I wished with all my aching heart
That she was with me.

Eifion Thomas

IN MY DREAM

In my dream I held you
ran my fingers through your hair
only to awake this morning
to find you were not there.
In my dream I touched you
whispered in your ear
held you tightly to me
together eased the fear.

In my dream I kissed you
softly on your face
then awoke this morning
in this god-forsaken place.
I my dream I saw you
laughing in the rain
playing like a child
free from all life's pain.

In my dream I loved you
no other love there'd been
but even before I woke up
I knew it was just a dream,
for in my dream I yearned for
to find the missing part
peace of mind, true happiness
contentment for my heart.

Paul Langley-Punter

YESTERDAY AND TODAY

Today and tomorrow
Is one you don't know
If you think
You're lost on the way
Think of today
Tomorrow
Is one you don't know
Yesterday and today
Today and tomorrow
With your love on the way
Is one you don't know
Today and tomorrow
Is one you don't know
Do you think of a girl
You'll meet on the way
Do you dream of a girl
You'll lose out on one day
Yesterday and today
Today and tomorrow
Is one you don't know
Do you go on through life
Do you think of one day
Yesterday and today
Today and tomorrow
Is one you don't know
Do you hope for a love
You'll find on your way
Well yesterday and tomorrow
Today and yesterday
Yesterday and today
Today and tomorrow
Are ones you don't know.

Barry Dillon

SINGLE BEDS

The imprint of my lipstick pinks his cheek.
My fingers soothe his face, his tousled brow.
I whisper words of love. He does not speak.
In sleep, he turns his back towards me now.
The ticking bedroom clock assaults my ear -
my open eyes resist all sleep, it seems.
But should he seek love's comfort, then I fear
to take my leave and to indulge in dreams.
I depart, with love's last, lingering kiss.
Cold, darkness wraps nocturnal arms around
my night-chilled, night gowned body. How I miss
the one who sleeps next door, without a sound.
Dry eyed, I doze - the trilling clock alarms.
I scoop my waking child into my arms!

Pauline Pullan

THE GIFT OF LOVE
(Dedicated to Mr G Knights)

G Give love and it will return to you,
E Ever escalating all life through,
R Run to grasp it, as it passes by,
R Retain it, and you will ask 'Why?'
Y You chose love, you have a gift beyond compare, and also 'I'.

Irene Greenall

FOR YOU

When you went so suddenly my love
To somewhere beyond the stars above
You left a gulf so wide
All feelings had to be denied.
Days to be endured
Nights of loneliness ensued
Life had no meaning
Just for sanity I was pleading.
But numb I could not remain
Not in yours my darling's name
No, life will never be the same
We must return from whence we came.
Living with the love that you created here
Guides me gently with less fear
I sense your presence like the brilliant sun
Engulfed in warmth till my days are done.
Then hand-in-hand we'll walk as planned
Forever in the promised land.

Gloria Hargreaves

FAREWELL

So now it's *our* farewell,
Our no more tomorrows,
Let there be no kisses in memorium,
Or broken-hearted tears,
Or forwarded venues with sentiment
Attached to this disunion.
And if ever we encounter more pain or sorrow or
Yearnings one for the other,
On a plain; dale or mountain that
We yet not know of,
We shall ignore all lost and future amours.
And even in our last adieus
From this earth that joined us
We shall not compromise
But close our eyes to die,
In the knowledge that this love died too.

S M Jackett

SAILOR

You belong to the sea,
Like the birds that ride her breeze, when she calls.
The silent beauty, a dormant mystery beyond compare.
Or the face of anger, destructive, vengeful, nature's dare,
And yet you long to be with her, when she calls.
Like the menagerie of creatures in her murky depths,
Those she has swallowed, her crevices holding their story,
And those she draws near, promises of excitement and glory,
And you long to be with her, when she calls.

You belong to the sea,
Oblivious to whether I'd die without you, of for you, she calls,
And you will follow, hungry for her power the humbling fear,
At the mercy of her kindness you say one more prayer,
And you long to be with her, when she calls.
You the ghost of my heart, its solace for you to be free,
And she will conjure her passion, to console, to be a friend.
She will not grow old or loose her charm, there can be no end,
And you long to be with her, when she calls.

You belong to the sea,
I gave the ultimate sacrifice to your sea that I abhor.
She claims her prize, her victory, she has you, you're unaware.
You'll never know my darling, of my love or how I care,
For you long to be with her, when she calls.
Treading your father's footsteps, being the man you must be,
And when she wraps you well in her calm, will you remember,
If carelessly she lets you rest, tell me, will you remember,
Still you long for her, not me, and she calls,

                    I'll never forget you.

Ruth

SPRINGTIME

Thirty years is more than half my life,
And yet when April comes again,
I think of springtime in another land:
A land of alpine meadows,
Of virgin snow,
A land of music.

There I found my love, a man of dreams,
Courageous in his quest for right,
Gentle to the weak, fond lover of mine:
All I had grown up to think
Was best, he was,
His love a treasure.

Separation too soon had to be,
His fears I failed to understand
And joyfully back home our love proclaimed:
No answering joy met mine,
Yet lifelong trust
Blinds our perception.

Father, dear, how could you watch my blank
Despair, those long, sad summer days?
It was from you, hero of my childhood
That my image of a man
Was perfect raised,
Innocent of fault.

Did you see pictures in the smoke plumes
As his letters burned? Our dream your
Prejudice destroyed, but time reveals past deeds:
And poured acid on my
Memory of you,
For many springtimes.

Rachel

THE WAY I FEEL

My heart stops, it misses a beat,
every time we do meet.
I want to sob, I want to cry,
this life I live is such a lie.
It's wrong to say 'I hate you',
I haven't the courage to say what's true.
In this poem I hope you find,
to my heart I ain't been kind.
You make me angry, you make me mad,
but most of all, you make me sad.
Why is it you are that way?
Why are my feelings so hard to say?
All I know is I miss you,
I only wish you had a clue.
I want to sob, I want to cry,
this life I live is such a lie.
To my heart I ain't been true,
I only wish I could tell you.

Janet Cross

ONCE UPON A MOONLIT NIGHT

Once upon a moonlit night,
two hearts did wander by,
radiating such true love,
beneath the moonlight sky,
beauty like I've never known,
beholden unto me,
compared to all there'd ever been,
this was ecstasy,
shallow breathing 'gainst my chest,
head laid next to mine,
arms that tenderly caressed,
bodies that entwine,
hearts that beat excitedly,
passion that's on fire,
and every tender loving kiss,
fills me with desire,
hands exploring every curve
of skin so soft as lace,
eyes that sparkle, illuminate,
the beauty of your face,
whispering so softly
the words, I love you so,
cherishing the moment,
over everything I know,
once upon a moonlit night,
so much love was made,
but were the feelings all for real,
or just a game we played?

Steve Eastwood

WHY DO I LOVE YOU?

You have to ask?
Spoil the moment.
But you have to ask. Why?
Not how much, or which way, but why?

It's down to chemistry, you could say
And save the technics for another day.
It's biological, zoological, human instincts, and all that jazz.
Magnetism . . . that sounds cool.
Physical attraction? But that's another tool.

Okay, I come clean, it's just the way it's always been.
That smile, the twinkle in your eye.
A grin, a look, and then the feelings start to rise

Something seems to move within.
A warm solution moving through the veins,
Always heading upwards.
The tingle starts as it reaches my head,
As the hairs on my neck almost reach for the sky.
A sparkle explodes inside my head,
And a contented smile comes to my face.

He's warm and tender.
He's funny and kind.
He's open and honest.
He's sincere and considerate.
He's gentle but firm.
He gets stressed but he's straight.
He gets sleepy and dependent.
He's a lover who enjoys my company,
And he tolerates my strange ways.

I love him to pieces in hundreds of ways,
And he can only ask . . . Why?

Pauline Bateman

I Was Blind

Don't give up your seat for me, I can easily stand.
You saw it first and fought bravely for it -
I do understand. I was once like you, a 'prisoner'
But then my eyes chose not to see.
I remember the blue and beige of Piccadilly Circus
When, in my rage, I ascended to the sound
Of voices: telling me that Green Park was closed.
When only my face told me of a breeze that bent over
The trees; to hear my secrets - then, as now, unseen.
For out of the tunnel the darkness closes in.
No familiar minding of the doors, or people pushing
Down inside in their irritated, silent din.
My journey was interrupted and it was fashionable
To despair. But then it was insignificant
And much easier to repair.

Mark Rasdall

VELVET ROSE OF LOVE

If good is white, and black is bad
What colour is love
Should it be pink or maybe peach
Like the fingers under your glove

You are the velvet Rose of Love
And the lily of my heart
You are the silver waters of ebony nights
And the greatest work of art

You are my first gold star at night
I'll be lost without you here
You're the one thing that keeps me smiling
Throughout cold days and nights

Your shining light keeps me so bright
You are my heart's desire
Your love flows gently on and on
Like the river flowing gently to the sea

You are the wings of an angel
The tide beneath my feet
You are my bird from heaven
The flagship of my fleet

Every smile reminds me of you
Dancing in silver moonlight
I sleep but my heart is awake
By the voice of love

You are but fair and pleasant
Golden delicious, sweet clementine
Let us go forth into the field
Come my beloved

Kelly Long (13)

LOVE AT FIRST SIGHT

When I saw you as you looked up
and I noticed you were smiling
and you liked the way I noticed
you were there.

When you saw me for the first time
and you noticed how I liked it
the way you smiled so long at me
that day.

How I loved you when I saw you
as the lights around us glistened
and the dancing all about us seemed so still.

How you loved me when you saw me
as the night came down and darkened
and the music all around us seemed to swell.

But you've gone now gone forever
and the night around me darkens
since I saw you for the first time that day.

Richard Stoker

DEAREST JOANNE

Hi there, my little, sweet, sexy lover,
Hope you're ok, and will one day discover . . .
My love for you is real, and will always be . . .
And we're going to last a long time, you'll see.
Things won't get worse, they'll only get better,
When you return, from being a jet-setter.
Our love will transcend . . . to a higher plain,
And we'll walk hand in hand, down Lovers' Lane.
I love you, I want you, I need you always,
Gone are my empty and unfulfilled days.
It's all because of you, I feel almost complete,
I will stick with you always, and never cheat.
Being with you - is always fun,
I often think about the things we have done.
One day I'm going to write a true love story,
About what it's like to see you . . . in all your beautiful glory.
It will be a best seller, without a doubt,
It will make all men scream and shout.
They will all want to experience you, but that can't be,
Because, Joanne, my love, you belong to me!
To finish off I'm sending you a thousand kisses,
In the hope that you, one day, will be my missus?
If this was to happen, all my dreams would come true,
Oh how good it is . . . to be in love with you.

Peter Dilworth

MY LOVE, MY HUSBAND

I sit all alone and think of thee
As you have left my side
They say you suffer no more
But nobody really knows
That you are at peace.

But I miss you my darling
As I sit here all alone
And think of the past
The love we had known.

When I first met you
We fell in love
Then before we knew
We had got married.

Then the little ones came along,
And now they have children of their own
But you my darling
Will stay forever in my heart
I will love you forever
When time comes we'll meet again.

M W Lowe

MY LOVE

The greatest pleasure and the deepest pain
The hardest loss and yet vast gain -
My love.
The richest treasure a soul can win
An ocean deep to revel in
Is love.

His anger and his pain is mine
He bleeds but the stain is mine
He's hurting, yet I bear the sign
When he has all forgot.

To see him smile, my greatest cheer
To be bereft, my darkest fear
It is enough when he is near,
My love.

Angela Hamer

An Oasis

To a man lost in the desert,
The sight of an oasis is absolute splendour.
The thought of a quenched burning thirst,
A satisfied hunger.
Relief from an endless searching,
Shade in the scorching heat.
Giving new strength to a tortured body,
Bringing vitality to a tormented soul.
Offering peace and serenity,
Gently soothing the pain.
Excitingly demanding,
Yet quietly yielding.
Like a man lost in the desert,
Like ice in the fire,
'You are like an oasis to me.'

Ashié Rana

MEMORIES

Those nights we had together
Stay unchanged with me forever
You know my feelings are the same
In my thoughts you will forever remain
Nights were young and so were we
This was meant, the way it had to be
And when we kissed and said goodnight
My heart was happy so full of delight.

And now you've gone and time stands still
In my heart I love you and always will
With hope my love, I may never forget
Neither the day nor the hour that we first met
I can hear the sound of loneliness
As I wrap around my dreams,
One day tears of rain will wash them clean
No more heartache, no more dreaming.
                    Precious,
                    Memories.

Graham Macnab

THE PARTING

No time now to kiss the snow-white head
Nor smooth the wrinkled cheek where once a peach did lay,
To hold the ravaged hand so gnarled and frail
To speak the tender words I always meant to say.

Blasé, I watched whilst age crept past
Assuming you, my rock, would ever stay.
Then in the night an angel called so quietly,
Peaceful and hushed to take my rock away.

No time this dawn to whisper gentle words of love,
To kiss the ear that listened to my woes,
But just to wonder where you sit above,
I want to know where all the angels go.

Yet can you hear the words I never said, or
See the tears traverse my fractured heart
And feel the guilt I feel, for came too soon
The voice above that called for us to part.

Though as I speak, a ray of sunshine gleams
A favourite rose, deep red, bloomed in the night.
The darkness that remains within my heart
Has seen its first and smallest chink of light.

Dare I to hope that this a message sent to
Let me know you feel my thoughts and pain,
A second chance perhaps to speak it in my prayers
A reassuring sign we'll meet again.

I'll send my love each morning and each night,
As my fractured heart heals, oh so slow,
Then I'll smile very soft at the scarlet red rose
For I know now where all the angels go.

Channon Cornwallis

NEWBORN

Breathless as I view
His gently sleeping form so new
Fragile fingers tiny toes
Rosebud lips and button nose.

Remembering the months gone by
Mixed up emotions made me cry
The numerous days spent feeling ill
A body ballooning against my will.

Waddling along - I couldn't walk
Baby arrived with 'gaga' talk
Exhaustion follows sleepless nights
No independence, no more own rights.

Thoughts of tiredness and despair
No time to myself and it's just not fair
And then I look into his eyes
A volcanic love makes me realise

There is no compliment so great
As seeing my partner reincarnate
No greater gift is there on Earth
Than the miracle called Birth . . .

Elaine Buck

FOR THE LOVE OF A CHILD

Gazing through the window, little children everywhere.
To remind me of the yearning that is in my every prayer.
I see a small child crying, wrapped in his mother's arms.
A protective shield around him as she keeps him safe from harm.
Will I ever know the love between a mother and a son
And be blessed with such a miracle? Please God just send me *one*.
So many times we've waited; we've waited and we've prayed.
We've hoped that 'maybe this time' but hope makes us so afraid.
My friends they all have children, my sister she has two,
And with pity in her eyes she says 'One day it will be you.'
We've seen so many doctors, looking on us in despair,
'Relax, let nature take its course' - This wait is so unfair.
We've had so many X-rays, undergone so many tests,
Tried experimental drugs and painful IVF.
Still nothing can we show, for the time that we have lost.
But the hope inside our hearts as we keep our fingers crossed.
We feel we're getting older, and time - it will not wait.
Our strength is with each other, only God knows of our fate.
I feel so very sick today. It's time to do 'that' test,
And I pray it won't be negative just as were all the rest.
He holds me in his arms as together we unite,
And vow whatever happens to continue with our fight.
All emotions shroud together - hope is on our side this time,
As through tears in my aching eyes, I see a faint blue line.

Carole A Taylor

GOLDEN WEDDING DAY

Our Golden Wedding Day, my dear,
Which we both did hope to share.
But God in his wisdom knew best,
That you could not be there.

Your sufferings are over,
And now you are at peace,
With our Great Creator,
Whose love will never cease.

Always in my heart
And in my mind,
Each day your love will be with me,
Us together it will bind.

Doris Fuller

GIVE ME THAT RIGHT

I will always love you dearly
Until the day I die
Always standing there beside you
Never making you cry
Always want you near me
Cuddle me so tight
Loving you forever
Please give me that right

I will give you all the loving
From the bottom of my heart
Together we will stand never more to part
Cherish you forever
Love you day and night
'Yes' cherish you forever
Just give me that right

Take the hand and heart I offer
The love that we can share
I offer my life to you
The love that it will bear
I need your loving kisses
The smile you give to me
Life would be so wonderful
If you gave that right to me.

P Carvell

I'll Be Home

Oh my darling I have missed you
Are you waiting there for me?
In my dreams at night I kiss you,
In your arms I long to be.

Oh my darling I am lonely
While we two are far apart,
In my thoughts I see you only
With your image in my heart.

Oh my darling I am burning
For your kisses face to face,
For our love will have no ending
When I'm locked in your embrace.

Oh my darling how I love you
And I hunger for your touch,
In the lonely hours of waking
I have longed for you so much.

Oh my darling don't forget me
Please remember all we shared,
Love and laughter, long caresses
For you know how much I cared.

Oh my darling I am yearning
To be home and by your side,
Now my travelling days are over
I'll be back to be your bride.

Betty Mealand

LOST TO YOU

Lost in your eyes
Caused my defeat
Kiss upon your lips
Tasted so sweet.

At your mercy
In fretful sleep
Your sweet caress
My heart begins to weep.

Gentle touch
Flares my mind
Wanting you so much
The tenderness so fine.

My pounding heart
Echo at night
Heavy eyes
Reflecting starlight.

Daily you return
When all alone
Together we learn
My heart begins to moan.

Nature speaks
In your smile so gay
Forever as one
In every way.

Held in my arms
Never letting go
Our love will always
Gently flow.

Bill Fulcher

MY ADAM

You think I can forget you?
My love, that is so untrue.
Could I forget to breathe?
My first and last thoughts
and *all* that goes between
are always of you.

I am the rib, you my Adam.
The woman taken,
bone of and flesh of you.
In the daytime my body embraces
the warm light -

This my love, my delight is you!

At night,
astir or slumbering
your essence cause me
to live the ecstasy we share.

Thoughts of you
softens my tone, my mood
and envelopes my voice with joy.
With you I am 'Dunns River Fall'.
You create
an aura
around my being
making me smile,
until all of me turns into laughter.
My equilibrium is poised exquisitely
within the gaze of your presence.

Without,
life is not,
no more

Rosetta Stone

LOVE'S LESSONS LEARNED

Courage mon brave
I know there isn't much to tell,
It all began
The very day you fell.

'Til then
You always rode another's heart,
Control,
It always played the biggest part.

You steered,
And the beast within obeyed,
You veered,
You lost the lead and strayed.

You're on strange ground
New territory here,
New fears abound
You've lost the reins I fear.

How easily
Love takes over our lives,
You're hooked
Your broken ego dives.

Think back,
Try to remember if you can,
The one you were
Before it all began.

Bobbie Dove

Watery Road

I kept my back globed away, so no one else could see.
Until you spoke, first time.
I turned, and fought against my shyness.

Watery road you are four years lost
I surfaced late, yet found your beauty.
Perhaps you have come to me, as I have come
To you - on a sea of could-be yearnings, a maybe swell of hope.

Present time throws up air, a fleeting gasp of air
The diver checks his aqua-lung
And through you, finds his breath.

David R Thompson

A HIGHLAND LOVE POEM

There is nane lad
Wid bear thee malice
Fate sang her ballant
Last fareweel - an oor
Paths lad
Aye Gaein tae sever
Grieves a lass
Fair an genteel
'Twas juist lad
Life's passing fancy
Yet remembrance
Do I hold dear
O' the pilbroch
Sweet purple heather
A pin o'gowd
An lover's tear

Irene Gunnion

AS TENDERLY MY THOUGHTS
(For Zoe)

As tenderly my thoughts
contour on to thee
I picture thee in my mind.
I see thy glorious smile,
and long to touch thy sweet warm lips.
I picture thee in full beauty,
for thou are beautiful.
As fresh as the dawn's dew is to blossoming tulips.
Thy soul is branded on to mine.
Thy heart liked with mine.
We are one, and forever shall be.

Raymond Mandeville

SPONTANEOUS ATTRACTION

When we first met
one fine spring day,
beams of light danced
between us, brilliant
as sunbeams on the
blade of Excalibur,
not just a spark of
chemistry but something
more than that, we were
closed in a magnetic
field of love at first
sight, as if predestiny
had folded us into
some enchanted womb
of our own, our feet
scarce touched the clouds
whereon we softly trod.
It seemed there were
a million suns in orbit
and never setting moons.

She put her hand in mine
as we journeyed to the stars.

Anna Punshon

COLD VALENTINE

Will you be my Valentine
Hold me close, love me, be truly mine?

February lingers cold like your eyes,
Blue light dancing through ice,
Looking the same in June's hot desire.
Where you walk winter light metamorphosises.
Your image clouds my imagination to all else.
Your lips warm me as your eyes lose me
Analysing unknown aspect of my soul.
Your smile tells of past loves lost,
Speak and you fill my listening soul
With your secret language of the heart.
Looking at you kaleidoscopes my senses.
You walk towards me painting yourself
In frosty air, to dream into my arms
And switch on your real world with a kiss.
Quickly you pull away from me,
Tears of pity wash the shores of your eyes
Breaking in sad tracks on your cheeks.

Will you be my Valentine
And with you coldness always be mine?

Mike Parker

The Sense Of Love

Almighty God, Loving Father, when we see the beauty of creation:
trees in autumn colours or
dark bare branches sprinkled with pure white snow,
a dew-drenched cobweb in the morning sun,
a snowdrop in January . . . a baby's first smile . . . we see love.
Thank You for sight, thank You for vision, thank You for love.

When we hear the wind in the trees,
the tide crashing ashore or lapping gently on the sand,
raindrops splashing in puddles . . . the song of the birds,
when we hear laughter or cries of anguish,
voices joined in prayer and praise; we hear love.
Thank You for the gift of hearing. Thank You for love.

When we smell primroses after an April shower,
violets, moss and trees,
a baby fresh from the bath . . . a loved one's favourite perfume,
we sense love.
Thank You for the sense of smell. Thank You for love.

When we hold a new baby, stroke our pets or
run our hands over smooth beautiful wood;
when we reach out to each other, in joy . . . or in sorrow
we feel love.
Thank You for the gift of touch. Thank You for love.

Loving Father God, when we use our senses
we see the wonder of creation,
we see You, we see Love.
Thank You for Love.

M Groves

YOUR NAME

I knew what I was doing
That left with you
I can't get out of bed now
I want to cry
Your name
I love you

The dewdrops on the evening air
shimmer as the light touches them
Your name
on their moist lips
I love
you I
love you.

The sunrise beckons and the sun pushes back
The heat of this pain will remain, justly, with you
I can't
win you
I have
lost you

I want you
but you've gone.

Rebecca Bennett

MY VALENTINE

He said that I would ever be
His one true love eternally
And that I was a pure delight
His angel lady of the night
He says I am his Valentine
His heart he says is always mine
Do I believe his words are true
Oh yes, oh yes, of course I do
My days with him are full of joy
'Though we're no longer girl and boy
There's something special, something fine
To be my darling's Valentine

Joan Fletcher

THE EARLY BIRD

From up above, the moon and stars did shine,
An evening, made for love, by Cupid's design,
I whispered softly in her ear, as our bodies did entwine,
She replied in her voice, so divine, 'Yes' the answer, I did seek,
'But St Valentine's Day is not until next week,' then placed a kiss
upon my cheek!

Benny Howell

MY VALENTINE

We met on a blind date
you took me to a dance
That night I had the feeling
this was a true romance

You said that you were shy
and couldn't ask girls on a date
Your one and only pleasure
was drinking with your mates

You said that meeting me was
the best thing in your life
and when you walked me home
you asked me to be your wife

After many years of marriage
and many more I pray
I'll always bless meeting you
on that Valentine's Day.

A Whyte

LOOKING BACK

'Twas February of 1959
I saw his smile, I read his sign,
I wasn't left in any doubt
I knew he'd come and ask me out

Six months on, I wore his ring
Together we did everything
All we wanted was to marry
So we decided not to tarry.

Into the bank our money went,
Nothing wasted, nothing spent,
We bought a house with one bedroom,
We didn't see the impending doom.

Our place we cleaned from end to end,
'Til the pressure was driving us round the bend
And then we had this awful row,
I can't remember the details now.

I took his ring from off my finger,
He went away, he didn't linger.
All he left me was a broken heart,
But everyone said I should make a new start.

Five years later I was at last made a wife,
And I've had many years of troubles and strife.
I lost my true love long, long ago,
And what I've suffered he'll never know.

So lovers out there, when your soul mate appears
Don't copy me, 'cos it'll end up in tears.
Live for each other, and always be happy
Get married for love to your wonderful chappie.

I loved him then, and I love him still,
And I know now, I always will.

Jaimi

FALLEN VALENTINE

The pub and club is where we met.
Holidays abroad we are all set
Off to Devon I am in heaven,
Move in her place!
Things moving at a quick pace!
I think we are ok of that there's no doubt.
Then she goes and chucks me out!
She spent all my money,
And that's no joke!
She's already got another bloke!
Never mind she will do well,
But I would like to see her
In ****** hell.

Ray Wilson

LITTLE ETHEL'S LOVE STORY

Little old Ethel heads for the door
She picks up the post from the mat on the floor,
A letter from cousin Nancy and the usual bills
She knows she's too old for a Valentine thrill

The frail old lady smiles to herself
Her friends were right she's been left on the shelf
She goes to the day centre with the usual crowd
Where the tea is weak and the music's too loud

The ladies dance the quick step together
The men sit and discuss the weather
As she settles into her favourite chair
Ethel straightens her dress and combs her grey hair

Now in her twilight years, she still has a grace
One of her smiles lights up whole her face
As the Tennessee Waltz begins to play
An elegant old gent walks her way

From behind his back he produces a card
Ethel stares at it long and hard
The words within are vibrant and clear
A message she thought she'd never hear

'Beautiful lady I see every week
I wait each time these words to speak
Would you fulfil an ambition of mine
And be my special Valentine?'

Ethel has been struck by Cupid's bow
She lets love in and feels its glow
The spring of life has finally sprung
And proves that love is not just for the young.

Sarah Peters

To My Valentine

Listen to my simple song
You loved me darling all day long,
With the sweetness of your smile
Always there in joy and trial.
Now you are no longer here
In the fusion of two minds,
Unexpected joy I find.
I'll love you for eternity
Until the day that smile I'll see.

Sheila Fernley Sing

TIME

I concentrated on my life.
Upon the future and the past.
Upon the present love affairs
And upon how long they'd last.
This is a question with no answer,
Nobody can say for sure.
I'm hoping it will last forever
But that's too much to ask for.
Oh! But this love is so wondrous,
Comforting and caring too.
I do have a fair idea
Of when I will stop loving you.
When the weeping willow weeps
And when the bluebell rings,
When the deaf man tries to hear
How well the dumb man sings.
When the snow's no longer white
And when grass isn't green,
When my feet are floating
On a breeze of silver sheen.
When the forget-me-not forgets
And when the sun won't shine,
I promise I shall love you
Until the end of time.

Louise Fleet

LOVE

Love is so important -
When tears are hard to bear -
And many times folk crumple
If there is no-one there to care.

It heals all the hurt and pain -
There is so much goodness in it -
And when a tunnel-light is seen
There is 'hope' to raise the spirit.

Love is such a soothing balm -
It's patient and so kind.
It is slow to anger
And it is 'caring' folk will find.

There are no conditions
And with sympathetic ears
Those with love can be ready
To wipe away the tears.

Whether man or woman
It's no shame to share a sad feeling -
For at times life gets one down -
The senses do start reeling.

Kind words will linger in the mind -
To the soul they are all feeding -
So share the love that you have
With those who are so needing.

Pat Melbourn

BLISS

This is heaven.
This is bliss.
It all started with a kiss.
Then, as passion reached its peak,
I could neither think nor speak.
Call it love
Or call it lust.
Call it anything you must.
Finally, I realise
How great it is to be alive!

Rosemary Thomson

LOVE IS . . .

Love's a constant friend
Who's at times demanding
Yet is patient and kind
With endurance everlasting.

She will wound you with her truths
In your quest to define her meaning
A never-ending cycle of continuous growth
A journey that's never ceasing.

She celebrates your triumphs
And is there for you in failure
Will be your strength in adversity
Her loyalty never wavers.

Love seeks nothing but love itself
And gives of itself completely,
Don't try to direct or steer its course
She'll guide you if she finds you worthy.

She'll be the water for your thirst and growth
And shears for your pruning
When you earnestly surrender, your heart will find its wings
Free to soar and experience all the revelations that she brings.

The faint-hearted will dance around her flames
To be entertained a bit,
But it takes a strong soul to be engulfed by her fire
And is purified and enriched by it.

Sonia Tennent

ALL IS HISTORY NOW

Love, came in the guise of his persistence
Her resistance, melted slowly
As snow on the hill.

Love, was offered swiftly on his part
Her heart, thought deeply
As waters in the ocean.

Love, formed the haven his arms brought
She caught, the moment gently
As summer rain on leaves.

Love, made the joy of his measure
Her pleasure, to share openly
As the bud turns to flower.

Love, was the reason given for his lie
She sighed, for the honesty
As a new baby smiles.

Love, mocked through his promise true
She knew, truth would evade her
As the rainbow's end.

Love, became mis-shapen in their head
Their bed, re-shaped the miracle
As the wind turns the cloud.

Love stormed in the anger of his fears
Her tears, washed away the cares
As the night clears the day.

Love, rebuked through the silence of his voice
She rejoiced, no more in her world
As the bereaved weep.

Love, only borrowed then returned sad with age
A page, that was written on
As the story end.

Jean Bishop

FIRST LOVE

First love remains crystal clear
And when each anniversary appears
I shed a silent tear.
Not one of sadness
But one of joy
Remembering the innocence
When girl met boy
Hand in hand, hearts locked
There was no key
And pledged wherever paths led
Wherever we'd be
That on Valentine's Day for a few moments
We'd rekindle our flame
By whispering softly
Each other's name.

Karen Forrest

VALENTINE '99

Who knows of love
Who never wrote
A single romantic line?
He plays at love
Who sends his love
A pre-printed valentine.

The emblem of lovers
An inspired line,
The excuse to cover
So many printed pages,
That lauded valentine.

It adds a little warmth again
To cold February
Those cards with romantic design
And a thousand requests
To be my valentine.

C O Burnell

TIME WARP

Our two hearts were born to meet and to fuse together,
To have and to hold in the time warp of love,
Which for such a brief time is sent from above
In many forms weaving the magic we seek.
Then having just found it, our short mortal span
Has finished and ended the race we both ran,
But our two hearts will beat in God's heaven forever,
If you will be my Valentine.

Paddy Jupp

CLICHÉS AT TEATIME

'Plenty more fish in the sea, my dear,'
She said, between mouthfuls.
As I brought up my late lunch
In a grief-soaked hanky.
Hung over eyes in red, blotched face.
And I wondered what a man might do,
If that was just a fish?
And decided that if she clichéd again
I'd ram that haddock down her throat
And then see how she felt . . . about fish.

Kürsté James

THREE STAGES

Young love can start
when you're just good friends
then suddenly a tiny spark
intensifies your emotions
holding hands is different and -
you're more conscious of your need
you experience a sense of expectancy
you didn't foresee
love that's based on passion alone
physically waiting to explode
like a cracker high up in the sky
then without warning
it fades away and dies
mature lovers that survive the years
don't rant or rave
nor stamp their feet
but wait patiently for another day
for experience has taught them
to be real lovers on Valentine's Day
you've got to give before you gain.

Chris Batley

ONE WISH, ONE DREAM

To have unity of souls, as love resides and shines sun over rain,
Child's innocence locked in a teardrop plea, to heal hatred
                                        and stop the pain,
Images of war, silent screams in the night,
If I had one wish, one dream, to make all the wrong Right.

When the shadows are broken and the vast sky is alight with rays,
A secret sign from God, if I could live that moment always,
When a Newborn breaks the silence or a solitary star shines its light,
To make everyone see the magic in life.

When fire and the ocean collide and dance with the tide,
When the sun embraces the moon and dusk hears the first bird cry,
When whispers follow butterflies on summer nights,
Gentle dreams, gentle wishes as hope takes its flight.

The belief and the faith every soul should possess,
Hearts never broken and tears never manifest,
Oceans will ease you, to change what you feel,
To have all hearts free and true if I had one wish, one dream.

Ciara Toal

You Said

You said you'd be my valentine
And give your heart to me,
A loving message on a card
Sent me into ecstasy.

You said our love would be forever
No one else would be the same,
And I believed you when you said
That I could take your name.

I started making wedding plans
And chose my bridal gown,
Of pearl-encrusted silk and lace
And veil soft as thistledown.

Red roses, sent with love you said
Which I nurtured with great care,
So why is it when I call you now
That you are never there?

Your card arrived this morning
It seems I've been mislead,
And all because I listened to
All the lies, you said.

Dorothy M Kemp

THE LADY VALENTINE

The Lady is my valentine
The Lady gave more than me
The Lady many wanted
The Lady who set me free
The Lady was always gentle
The Lady was my soul
The Lady I never loved well enough
The Lady of Valentine role
The Lady tried the hardest
The Lady was light and bright
The Lady I never got to know
The lady deserves Mr Right
The Lady never was my Lady
Yet I burn for that to be so
The Lady had a special gift
The lady could melt the snow
The Lady never angered
The Lady was a dream
The Lady I took for granted
The Lady who swims the stream
The Lady My Lady Our Lady
The Lady of Love you are
The Lady of all the virtues
The Lady I love from afar
The lady any man would cherish
The Lady ahead of her time
The Lady many would die for
The Lady Valentine.

James Stott

BROKEN

In the silence of this room, with no TV, radio or remote control,
I sit and watch my reflection in the mirror
                              he once made for me,
Mosaic pieces, broken colour, a daisy in each corner.
My face is disappearing
                    And still downstairs they scream.
It's 1am. I should sleep, but still I sit here still,
Friend who understands this moment with me,
I stand with you in the curved moonlight,
I walk with you through the dark, wet grass,
                    Exchanging deepest heartfelt all.

Saba Zai

UNTIL ONE DAY

I see her face in sunshine,
I see it in the rain.
I long to hold my angel
and I never will again.

I knew when I first met her
when we were eight years old,
that she would be my wife one day
to love, to have, to hold.

Valentine's Day, ten years ago
the man who took her life,
also stole my hopes and dreams
the day he took my wife.

Oh, my sweet love, I long to say
how much I love you still.
I wake each morning, sleep each night
loving you until . . .

Until, one day my heart is stilled
and again we can be one,
and I can cry, my valentine
I come, my love, I come.

T Alexander

SILVER ANNIVERSARY

Twenty-five years, the Silver,
Wedding, Anniversary,
How the years have,
Gone, through happiness,
And love, and laughter.

We had no children,
But happy with our,
Careers, and our,
Lives together,
We will celebrate,
in our own usual way.

A special dinner,
And a taste of wine,
We will be together,
For another twenty-five years,
I can see it,
All, through my,
Tears, Oh dear,
Not me, these years.

Barbara Brown

VALENTINE LOVERS

When first he sent a Valentine
I did not know that he'd be mine.
Edged with lace, beflowered, it
Encompassed love, kindness and wit . . .

Our future life was wreathed in mist
Although our lips we both did kiss,
For there were those who wore a frown
And tried to tug our romance down.

Mixed religions, they all swore
Would bring disharmony to our door.
We listened with our ears half closed;
Nonetheless he then proposed.

Our faces both were sights to see
For we did wed, my sweetheart and me.
Love and stubbornness were the tools
To show dissenters who were fools . . .

The smiles we wore then can still be seen
And what an adventure in-between!
We've laughed and we've cried and sometimes been sad
But both are so thankful for all that we've had.

Our union was blessed with progeny, three,
Beloved sons for him and me.
This autumn, a toast! - *Fifty* years together
Trust, humour and love have been our tether.

Joy Lennick

THE KISS WILL BE IN PARIS

It was in the dream of Valentine
Where once our love was born
A dream trusted to eternity
Unto which our oath was sworn

In our hearts there lived a promise
A kiss reserved for a special place
A legacy left by destiny
That both our spirits chase

Thus our fate belonged to valentine
To the bards of romance and myth
The dream will be our moment
And this evening shall be our kiss

The stars awake like lovers' eyes
Their romance is our champagne
We are flowers in the garden of heaven
Watching the moonlight kiss the Seine

We will be the heart of valentine
And love will be our tune
The kiss will be in Paris
'Neath the shelter of the moon

David Bridgewater

LOVE GEMS

Garnet, compassionate warm and inviting
Red is the ruby passionate and exciting
Lustrous like a pearl, its luminous shine
Mellow as amber in all its finery

Jealousy and envy within emerald green
Sapphire, soft velvet, shiny blue sheen
Deep as the ocean, colour aquamarine
Topaz, transparency bewitch and demean

Opal, its mystery serene and aloof
Unlucky in love, betrayal of truth
The gemstones of love, two hearts that are captured
A diamond forever, is true love enraptured

Rosemary-Elaine Humphrey

THE MECCA MILE

I've always travelled to your lane
Because I love you so;
Your self-sufficiency gives pain,
I've loved you long ago.
I'm old to be a Juliet
To casual Romeo
But, dear sweet friend, I love you yet,
I do adore you so.
Climbing of hills makes heartbeat fast
Yet fool I travel on,
Cannot resist that spell you cast,
All stupid pride has gone.
I laboured every month this year,
Appalled because I'm slow;
I love you but we don't live near,
Too bad! I love you so.
I've trembled at the thought of loss,
Bless aura that you throw,
Still I came, did not care a toss,
I've always loved you so.
I've noticed we are growing frail,
Get weary when we speak,
Through stressful times I did avail
Myself of you each week.
Opportunities beckon still,
I'm slowing down, I know;
I wonder if this new year will
Match last, I've loved you so.

Ruth Daviat

VALENTINE LOVERS

Real love is heaven-
sent -
Love is a life's commitment.
Some of us have not yet found -
So I live in hope!

I have friends and then we part -
These are not from a love from the heart -
We can sometime find this mystery -
So I live in hope!

So Valentine's Day will be here soon -
Could Cupid point his arrow in my direction?
They say love is there from the start -
So I live in hope!

My friend told me no lies -
Her Valentine - he died -
But yet her love for him went on -
Forever she would love her Ron.
So I live in hope!

One day it could come along -
I had known many men in the past -
But how great to meet one that would last -
So I live in hope!

I'd love to suffer ever pain, envy, heartache -
They say that's Love! that will really last -
Then we would be Valentine Lovers -
So I live in hope!

Margaret Evelyn Smith

SPECIAL LOVE

A special love to last my life
The special love of a good man's wife.
To feel the nearness in his arms
Listening to his sweetened charms.

That's my special love, my special dream
When the man I love is all he seems.
The love in my eyes will not grow dim
And in my heart is only him.

When I see him I feel nothing but calm,
Knowing with him I'll never know harm.
Togetherness we'd have every day
Especially at night when together we lay.

What will come from this wonderful match?
What beautiful thoughts will my heart unlatch?
This special love of a dreamy state
Can only in wonderment now create.

Denise Shaw

A VALENTINE HEART

A valentine heart
Is a heart full of love
It's as if it's been sent
From God's heaven above
It cannot be compromised
Broken or torn
I believe it was waiting
For you to be born
To live with you
As you saw each blessed day
And blossom to find me
Whatever the way
And found, I was captured
By its burning light
To think of you constantly
Daytime and night
To realise you were
My one heart's desire
Whose kiss was the torch
That ignited my fire
Whose love would encompass
And totally care
In times when I'm lost
In my darkest despair
This love has no boundaries
Nobody can part
It's a love only found
In a Valentine heart.

David Whitney

THE RING

Placed on the table,
As another blue wave meets
From the corner of eyes
I've tried so hard to compete

Cold by the window
Still warm from a touching hand
A kiss from the sea breeze
You tried so hard to understand

Left in the sunlight
Silent by the sad sea
From the corner of eyes
You said this would be easy

Footprints on the sand
Holding hands a golden touch
Another blue wave meets
Words have never said so much.

Lefort

FOR YOU - MY VALENTINE

I bring you everything I have to offer,
A heart so full of love it overflows,
A thousand golden arrows pierce its centre,
Fired from a thousand Cupids' golden bows.

A pocket full of sunshine brightly shining,
Waiting to pour out its warmth on you,
Surround you in its ever glowing splendour,
To light your path wherever you might go.

A basket full of rainbows cross your heavens,
To fill your skies with colours every day,
Multi-coloured, iridescent beauty,
To lead you onwards, guide you on your way.

A bouquet full of happiness and laughter,
Blooms of such splendour you have never seen,
Filling your senses with sweet scented perfumes,
Perfection, as befits a perfect Queen.

A treasure chest of memories we are sharing,
Diamonds, rubies, sapphires, emeralds green,
Pearls and gold and silver, beyond value,
Such priceless gems that no one else has seen.

I would row a boat across the oceans,
Through roughest storms against the tide of life,
Carrying these gifts, this bounty that I offer,
Laid at your feet for you, my darling wife.

James W Sargant

MY ETERNAL LOVE

I have waited an eternity in hope of finding the perfect love,
But what I have found isn't what I was expecting,
It is something which is, and always will be, beyond my
                                                wildest dreams,
It is a love which I know has travelled from the deepest depths of
                                                my heart and soul.

A love which wells up inside my chest and makes me ache all over,
I have met my perfect partner and I hope I can be with you forever,
Someone with unbelievable qualities which constantly amaze me,
When I'm away from you it feels as if something has taken away
                                                my whole reason for living,
Without you I can't breathe, I'm like the earth with no sun to show
                                                me the way.

When I look at you I see that you are full of love and caring,
A love and caring that you give me in such a way it is impossible
                                                to explain,
When I find you next to me in a morning, I just want to hold you
                                                close to me and never let you go,
You'll never know what a feeling you give me knowing that we
                                                belong to each other.

Although we have not known each other long, I feel as if we have
                                                been together forever,
I would sacrifice everything I have, even my life just to be with you,
But what I want to say is this, I am yours and I always will be yours
                                                for eternity,
But also I want to say is that I truly love you.

Mark Davidson

VALENTINE'S DAY

It's Valentine's Day on Sunday
What do you think I'll get?
Flowers, chocolates, underwear?
Love? Do you want to bet?
You see I've been married for 15 years
And romance is quite dead
He doesn't see me anymore
Not even in our bed.
Oh we have sex when he's in the mood
It doesn't last for long
And if I'm silent afterwards
He doesn't ask 'What's wrong?'
He never listens to what I say
He doesn't even look
After all I'm just the servant here
The cleaner and the cook
He never holds my empty hand
Or looks into my eyes
But maybe now on Sunday
My spirits they will rise
When I come down to breakfast
There will be a big surprise
There will be a single blood-red rose
Nestling by a cup of tea
And just a note in his neat hand
Saying how he loves just me
Now my eyes are full of sparkle
At the thoughts I am evoking
Could this happen on Valentine's Day
'You must be ruddy joking.'

Jan Price

IMPRESSIONS OF THE FIRST LOVE

In years gone by
We all loved to try
To make a friend for life
Someone to help when in strife
The first love had to be
Someone special just for me.

A Valentine card sent
I knew what it meant,
From someone unknown
He was not alone
But for half a century
That was most unlikely.

His life is complete,
With grand-children sweet.
As I have too
So what could I do?
Life is for living,
Loving and giving.

A Joan Hambling

NEVER FORGET

Even though there's times you feel
Unloved, alone that life's unreal.
Never forget that you're never alone
And you are loved you've always known!

Why question what you know to be true,
And doubt all that was spoken to you.
Don't you remember the words that I love you
Your reply was I love you too.

Never forget our love is genuinely real.
Our love is promised, blessed and sealed.
Always remember you were told from the start
That you and me would never part.

You know you mean so much to me,
Our love will dwell through eternity.
There is happiness every day,
Remember I promised I'll never sway.

Never forget that I love you too
You're what I wanted and this is true,
Please remember I fell right from the start,
And promised that we'd never part.

Caroline Rowe

THE LONELINESS OF NOWHERE TO GO!

Two people undervalued,
Rejected, underrated,
She addict walking tightrope of death,
He schizophrenic wishing to draw last breath.

Each of their lives, comfortless,
Cheerless,
No kin that cared, friendless,
Emptiness!

Their sad nomadic paths crossed,
Hauling each other from dross,
He helped her off drugs, watched day and night,
She checked he had jabs to be free from his blight.

At homeless hotel on coast,
Wan ghosts,
Gazed at sea farthermost,
Thoughts engrossed.

Once he bought petrol, struck match,
Despatch!
God grasped him, doused despatch,
Eyes unlatch!

Now he loves her, she loves him,
Nevermore forlorn victim,
Living in God's light, not twilight dim,
Found each other, nature's simple life and Him.

Aiming to a new skyline
With their loving Valentine.

Hilary Jill Robson

UNTITLED

Come into the sea
Naked and dark into a darker sea
If language were water
We'd be lost under the weight
Of our words unspoken

Like the beauty of decay
I trace with my finger the
outline
of your mouth like a
slow perversion

I burn myself in your eyes
And run through everything you are
Let's dive and
disappear
To an island out of reach.

Deborah Counter

HOPE FOR ALL

Relationships end, emotions mend
Stand alone for growth spiritually sends
Look within to find oneself
Heart and mind combined to seek truth
To stay clear of others' ruthless manner
Hope for all seeking purposeful goals
When earned stability in control
Which won't forlorn
Future love meant to warm.

Alan Jones

LOVE AND MEMORY

There, in the room of new promise,
I met her ghost -
Hair and brow spoke of tender old moments,
when pink flowers and white veil
drowned me, happily, in 'I will'.
Lips and cobbled skin,
glowing like rare eggshell,
admonished my memory for
bruising her legs in horseplay
(then after, her coy smile,
when she delighted to entice
by still raising her skirts,
though the bruises had gone).
Bright, deep eyes, like electric stars,
sang words of love:
love that painted my every move,
through thoughtless times,
heartache and pain,
binding it all in gold.

I am haunted in this warm room;
but she enters behind me.
We gaze together at the small child
- Fruit of trust;
Chubby fingers holding firmly
to the ghost of love and memory,
and never letting go.

Duncan L Tuck

VALENTINE LOVERS

How many Valentines will I receive this year?
Perhaps one from Alan who is a perfect dear
Or Philip with his star shining eyes
His broad smile that brightens my skies

Terence with his cheeky 'come hither look'
He really is a handful to manage in my book
Yet again perhaps Darren with his fair hair so curly
He merely nods with a pink face smile

Full of himself Alexander, a likeable workmate
Well, he certainly takes the cake,
He pinches my bum whenever he passes by me
That's rather rum; yet I giggle with glee!

I can hardly wait for Valentine Day
My brain is bursting at the seams
I must keep it at bay for the umpteenth time
Oh! How many will there be, enough to write a rhyme?

When Valentine Day dawns
I will arise and be waiting the delivery of the pawns
Red heart-shaped letters I hope will arrive galore
Pushed through the letter box by the postman onto our hall floor!

To my great surprise I opened them all
Not one's writing did I recognise I recall
Except for one he never has changed his style
Of writing, it was from my dad, my everlasting Valentine lover!

Alma Montgomery Frank

THE LOVER BEHIND THE BRUSH
(For Helen)

Poetry is my paint,
The unwritten word
Is my canvas,
My soul is my pallet
And my heart
Is my brush,
So I am
The artist,
You are my
Model
And love
Is my
Art.

Ian Simandl

TILL DEATH US DO PART

'With this ring I thee wed,
With my body I thee worship
And with all my worldly goods I thee endow';
And from this day forward
I will crush your spirit with my personality,
I will make your life bitter, twisted agony,
We will argue and fight till death us do part.

I will give you children to raise your hopes
And they will turn and dash them thoughtlessly to the ground,
I will kill your dreams, demolish your trust,
I will sever you from former loves
And put nothing in their place,
I'll show your love to be totally unfounded,
And still it will not be the end.

Till, between us we will destroy
Ourselves, each other.
And when the fight is gone from us
And we live side by side in oblivion,
We will both be unrecognisable
As the two who set out together, in hope,
Thinking ours was the only love in the world.

V J Sutton

ANOTHER VALENTINE

Another Valentine
and love's still mine.
This wonderful dream we share.
With love in my heart
the greater part
belongs to you.
With you there
I'll always care
and have great company.
The love we feel
a kiss will seal
adding a hug for good measure.
Along this path
you make me laugh
simply because you love me.
This love we share
is so rare,
we are always here for each other.
The scent of your hair
your secret touch
it's wonderful to be loved by you so much.
The longer we live
the more we can give
to please one another.
This love will grow
from the seeds that we sow,
cherished by loving hands.
With a song in my heart
we promise never to part,
now until forever, love, please stay.

Rosemary Medland

Love Is ...

Love is like a flower in full bloom,
　Dancing, kissing in the light of the moon,
Radiant, shining like a brand new star.

Love is like a rainbow, splendid, bright.
　When you can't bear to part at night.
Hoping, praying, that love won't die.

Love is like a raindrop, there is nothing as pure.
　Love is a feeling no-one can cure.
Love is a caress, gentle and warm.
　Love is the softness after the storm.

Deanna L Dixon

LOVE'S REDEMPTION

The power of your love was made so clear in that you allowed your
son so dear,
To be hung on a cross, be crucified, our debt to pay, our death to die;
So vast is your love, so great the tide, that you took the stripes all in
your stride,
You took all our pain and our disease and brought us healing and peace;
So strong is your love it never fails, even when our love grows cold
and fails,
You remain faithful, you remain true, and Lord Jesus that's why
I love you!

Julie McKenzie

GOOD TIMES GONE

Out for a drink, after our work; up on a binge, we've got a nerve
Threw me a wink, but I looked like a berk; all my hair singed
In the dark where one lurks.
Cash in the gamble, luck's not on our side; with my life a shambles
there's nowhere to hide.
Win a game of plain pool, but I'll remain the drunk fool; naively I still
believe that she may still love me.
Golden good times gone, as on comes our song
I get up and dance, as on me lights shone
the dance floor's all mine, while the pride is all yours
I know I'm not perfect, we all have our flaws.
You say I'm not worth it, now gone's the last straw
but don't I deserve it? Only wanting some more,
So I respond with the phrase - darling, make love not war.
Waste my limited winnings as I'm stood at the bar
I ain't got a girl, nor a house, crashed new car
Up to now I've got nowhere, yet I've travelled so far
As you laugh in my face, things aren't that funny - Ha! Ha!
Put on some 'throwaway' music, and tentatively tap to the beat
Get out of my way is put nicely, because you're caught up under
my feet.
Don't tell the whole world, instead be as possible discrete.
You say I've made a mess, and through the window thrown neat.
Your round, you're shot, my town - well it's not;
You're crowned but forgot, life's worth such a lot
And love - I'm afraid, very rarely comes easy.

Stephen Rudd

THE DEATH OF LOVE

Once Upon a Time, I fled
From you, with our two kids, instead
Of enduring threats and blows,
Insane rages. Goodness knows
What might have happened had we stayed.
'Treat 'em mean'! The game you played.

I entered a safe, quieter scene.
Forgot the hell of what had been,
And spent what seemed eternity
Being, simply 'Mother-Me'.

One day, my daughter, now full-grown,
Divorced and also on her own,
Told me, for her peace of mind
She absolutely *had* to find
Her father, learn what made her 'tick'.
My world dissolved. I felt soul-sick,
Self in smithereens, although
I knew I had to let her go.
Give my blessing, block the fears,
Somehow stem the rush of tears.

She visited, but found you dying.
'Dad loved you, Mum.' She told me, crying.
You begged her for a note from me
To help you pass on peacefully.

Coda

I asked for strength from 'Up Above'
Then wrote: 'My once and only love . . . '

Elizabeth Mark

THROW ME A LIFELINE

I listen with all good intentions
And smile with sympathy
You tell me of your expectations
I accept them happily.

Yet in my heart it isn't right
Your words mimic my pain
I suffer endless sleepless nights
I find it all a strain.

I hurt with such intensity
With pain I thought I'd lost
And like old ghosts it haunts me.
Is loving you this cost?

I don't want love second-hand
I've walked this path before
You know how well I understand
But I am needing more.

As we turn this round and round
I think with passing time
That you will let me slowly drown
Please, throw me a lifeline.

Lynne Morris

HAPPY VALENTINE'S DAY

Will you be my Valentine
Today and evermore?
This we will never know!
As you are with the one you love
And I am also betrothed.
Never mind we can just look
And know that it's not to be.
But have a happy Valentine
And always think of me!

Chris Blowman

ENVELOPED

The moment I lay down in bed
Thoughts of you, they fill my head
I close my eyes, the scene begins
I drift away with dreamer's wings.

I picture you - you're always there
Your tender smile, your tousled hair
Your arms are never far away
They wrap me up, and there I stay.

Greedy lust absorbs my skin
Potent love, it glows within
My heart takes on a faster pace
I'm enveloped, our limbs embrace.

Morning comes, I reach for you
You kiss my eyes, I kiss you too
My dream becomes reality
Your eyes and skin delight in me.

I bless the day that you were born
If you should die, my soul would mourn
For you, my eyes will always shine
For I am yours, and you are mine.

Fiona L Harden

THOUGHTS OF YOU

Your face, the thought of your face,
and my heart begins to race.
All it takes is just a smile,
and I feel alive, just for awhile.

A lot of words can be spoken in a 'Hello',
and my heart does not feel so low.
And if by chance,
I turn, I may see you glance.

Watching you from a distance,
I often feel in a trance
and as I try to send my thoughts to you,
then, maybe I won't feel so blue.

You've wove a web around my heart,
I pray you won't tear it apart.
The wheel of life keeps turning,
And for you, I'll never stop yearning.

Janet Lawreniuk

MY LOVE

I saw you across the classroom.
Those twinkling blue eyes,
and that soft brown hair.
You turned around and saw me there,
and all I could do was stand and stare.
My legs went weak,
My heart missed a beat
and I thought this was love at first sight.
I waited for you to come over,
Days went by and so did months,
I decided I'd talk to you
And that's just what I did
We talked, laughed and joked,
And it was great
Until you spoke of Maria,
Maria this Maria that.
I was speechless,
And the pain was so bad,
It broke my heart and blew my mind.
You were my Romeo,
But I wasn't your Juliet.
Love is a two-way thing,
And this just wasn't love

Zahra Jiwa

VALENTINE'S WISH

I do not know if you received the message I got of love
Long-lost and best forgot

Looking for a new love is so very hard to find
I wish I was back with my one and true love
I long left behind

Alas she long passed away and that
I find so hard to bear
Will I ever find a new love so rare for me to share

I see love all around me, I see love everywhere I go
The love of life. The love of God
But the love of a woman is what I have not

To be her Valentine, and drink the wine that makes her mine
Beauty within that only lovers can begin to share

But day by day I sit and pray of love on Valentine's Day
A love that seems so very far away and I can't seem to find
The words that could make a woman mine

Life so empty and bare without a love to share
No Valentine's card will I become, and one more year no card to
be sprung
So all you people out there that have a love so true to share
Be sure to show them how much you care

Paul Volante

FIRST LOVE

The school bell rings, class is over for the day,
Pupils jostle for the door, pushing anyone in their way
Friends call to me to hurry but I'm not eager to join them yet
I hang behind excitement building, for soon I'll see my love, my pet.

Everyone's gone now, the cloakroom deserted
Perched on the sink and craning my head
I can get a good view of the senior boys' bike shed
Heart pounding, pulse racing, stomach like lead.

Through the window I see him, a vision in blue
Oh, how I love him if only he knew
For weeks now I've watched him my love grows and grows
I'm certain he'll love me as soon as he knows.

My senses all tell me to rush to him now
Declare myself completely and give my solemn vow
That our love will last forever no other shall turn my head,
I'm coming my love, wait, wait, until it's said.

Just as I'm shuffling to jump from the sink
Through the window I see her, a vision in pink
She runs to my love with arms open wide
He waits to embrace her, I stay inside.

I watch them embrace, tears stinging my eyes
How could he betray me, not hear my tortured cries
My heart is broken, I'll never love again
My life is over at the tender age of ten!

Pauline Mary Tarbatt

UNTITLED

Beauteous rose
whisper your secret in mine ear,
Your fragrance doth reveal
a message I must hear:
Convey to him, your secret, whom
I love . . .
And overpower his heart,
His sensuality,
Your fragrance born of smouldering passion
It will be
A potent elixir for one
I love:
Enfold him in the sweetness of
Your fragrant power,
About his body
Thus entwined with mine each hour,
And we will share your secret with
Our love . . .

Carolyn Smith

THE FORCE OF FEELING

As though a magnet is at work,
Their eyes are drawn to meet,
And there remain, locked in that gaze,
Feeling at home, feeling complete.

They make pleasant conversation,
Hopefully uninterrupted,
Willing this moment to last,
Never to be disrupted.

Another speaks and the force is broken,
Their eyes are forced to separate,
To look upon the one who has spoken,
Only to resume, a new gaze to create.

Their eyes communicate again,
She is lost in the pool of his pupil,
And as he is drowning in hers,
The feeling is so very mutual.

Sharon Thone

VALENTINE'S DAY

The need of love is nature's bent.
For husband, lover, wife, or friend.
It runs our life
Fulfils our needs
So Valentine's Day just sets the seeds.
A day to ponder on our lives
With so much trouble, so much strife.
But love is strong,
It ties
It binds
It comes in many different kinds
A hug - a kiss
Won't go amiss
Valentine's Day is the time for this.
So now in nineteen ninety-nine
Let's see if everything goes fine

Jeffrey Shedlow

VALENTINE LOVERS

Will you be my Valentine and
wear my diamond ring?
Will you swear to love me as
winter turns to spring?
I promise to be true to you for you're
my heart's desire
I love you more each moment -
My heart alight with fire.
Could you love me as I love you?
Oh please say 'You'll be mine'
Then we can plan our wedding day
my sweetest Valentine.

Mary Monica Cookson

A VALENTINE

To my Valentine my husband,
Go thoughts of tongue and pen.
Now of forty years or more
A prince among most men

Over all the years and time.
Over all the ups and downs.
The sorrows and the joys thereto.
The laughter and the frowns.

You'll always be my Valentine
Till the end of all our days.
My dear devoted Valentine.
I love you dear always.

Jean Turner

ADOLESCENT ADORATION

If only he could hold in check
the rush of thoughts that trip
his words
to make them sprawl, so clumsily.

All that he says reflects unease,
desire to please frays sentences:
unstrung, they scatter into air,
whirl there, with meaning lost.

Is this the sum of loving her,
- the end before a futile start?

In mood of sudden, mute despair,
he leaves,
to tend his grieving heart.

But now, at last, the time is right
to set strong feelings
on the line:
'word perfect' is the card he's
found
to woo his distant Valentine.

June Burden-White

TRANSIENCE

Happiness is transient.
Feel it in the movement of the dance
before the pain of the stretched muscle
hear it in the silence between
the notes of the symphony;

In the dark of a star-lit
sky, when I hear you breathing -
happiness when I touch you
my lover, beloved;
In the green leaves of changing
seasons

       hold me beloved, lover.
Imagine you
near . . . happiness as intangible
transient, light as
sting of the guitar, to dream in
your eyes,

this stillness touching my soul.
I weep. To reach for you,
lover, beloved, and never know.

L A Churchill

UPDOWN

For four years,
I go down the village street.
You come up the village street.
Seeing you I feel *up* while you seem *down.*
Sad-eyed aura and profound beauty transfixes me.
I never chat much to you (I have a girlfriend),
And upheaval could only ensue,
Because I will fall in love with you.

I hope that woman is cherished,
By someone, think I.

Comes a time,
My girlfriend and I no more rhyme.
You'll be mine.
I pursue some chatting.
We get on extremely well,
So well that you feel that you can tell me,
Intimate things, on the phone one night.

'I've just fallen head-over-heels,
In love with someone,
Out of the blue!'
Yes yes yes but I mustn't get excited,
I'm just trying to get to know her.

It's a friend who I've known a long time,
And it just happened.'
Four years, yes, yes . . . up up up.

'His name's Pete'

No, no my name's Frank!

Such good friends have we become,
That I say *I'm very happy for you!*

Down down down . . .

Steve Taylor

SUBMISSIONS INVITED
SOMETHING FOR EVERYONE

POETRY NOW '99 - Any subject,
any style, any time.

WOMENSWORDS '99 - Strictly women,
have your say the female way!

STRONGWORDS '99 - Warning!
Age restriction, must be between 16-24,
opinionated and have strong views.
(Not for the faint-hearted)

All poems no longer than 30 lines.
Always welcome! No fee!
Cash Prizes to be won!

Mark your envelope (eg *Poetry Now)* **'99**
Send to:
Forward Press Ltd
Remus House, Coltsfoot Drive,
Woodston, Peterborough, PE2 9JX

**OVER £10,000 POETRY PRIZES
TO BE WON!**

Judging will take place in October 1999